THE CHURCH'S FOUNDATION:
Peter Steps Up in Faith

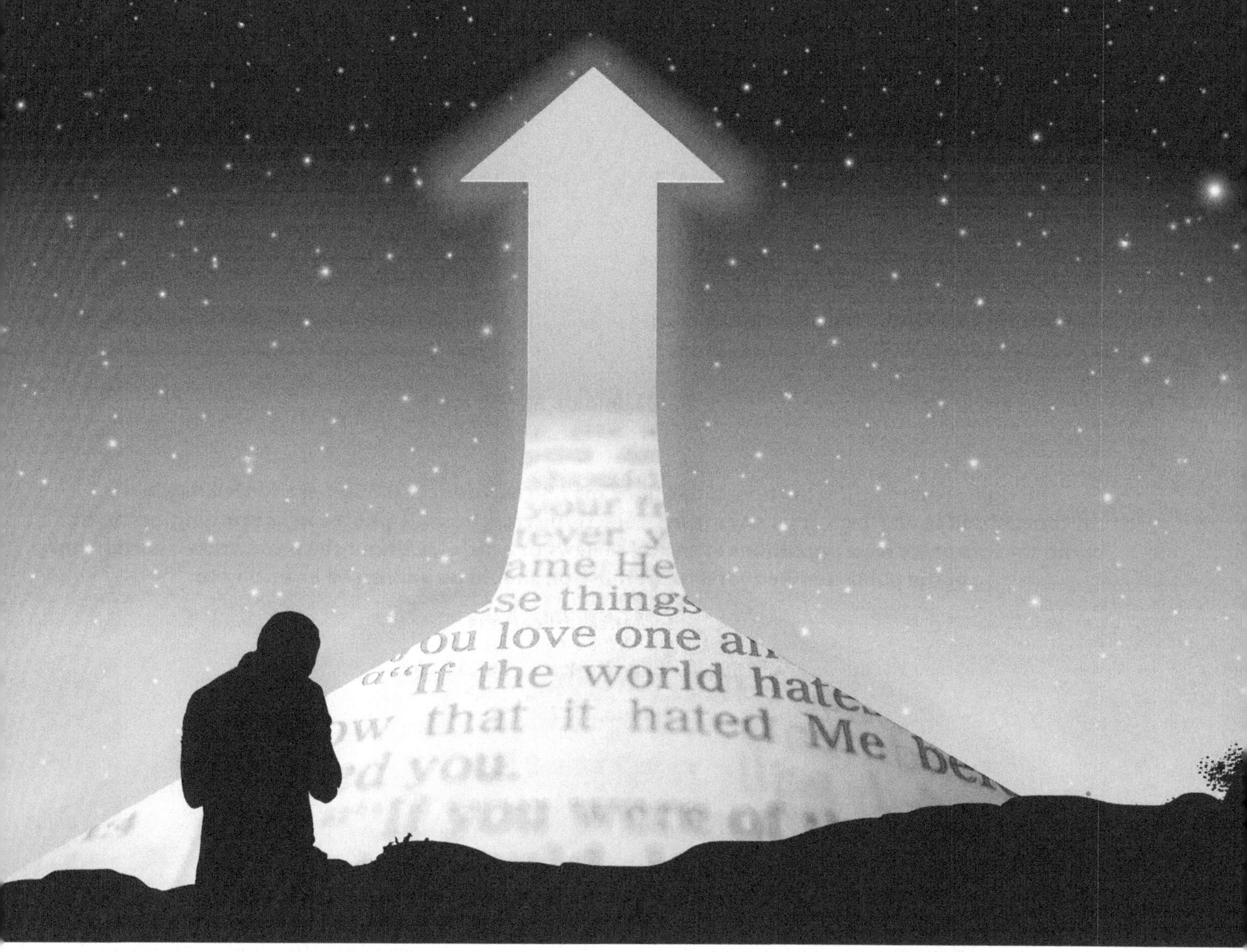

© 2024 LifeMark Ministries

All rights reserved. No portion of this book may be reproduced, stored in a retrieval system, or transmitted in any form or by any means – electronic, mechanical, photocopy, recording, scanning, or other – except for brief quotations in critical reviews or articles, without the prior written permission of the publisher. Requests for permission should be addressed in writing to:

LifeMark Publications

2001 W. Plano Parkway, Suite 3403

Plano, TX 75075

ISBN: 978-1-944058-20-3

Scripture quotations marked (NIV) are taken from the Holy Bible, New International Version®, NIV®. Copyright © 1973, 1978, 1984, 2011 by Biblica, Inc.™ Used by permission of Zondervan. All rights reserved worldwide. www.zondervan.com The "NIV" and "New International Version" are trademarks registered in the United States Patent and Trademark Office by Biblica, Inc.™

Design by Angeline Collier / Halo Creative
www.halocreative.com

Peter Steps Up in Faith

It's hard to imagine what it was like for the first Apostles over 2,000 years ago.

They'd followed a Jewish carpenter for 3 years - constantly being Amazed by his Teaching and his Miracles. No one had ever taught what he taught and the way he taught. No one healed people, cast out demons and brought the dead back to life like he did - and yet most people didn't accept him.

The established religious leaders saw him as a threat - and he was. Government officials were afraid of him for the influence he had on the people - also true. But, what about those closest to him - put yourself in their sandals.

The Teaching - a New Kingdom, a New Way, etc. was hard to grasp. And, Miracles were hard to believe - calming a storm at sea, feeding 5,000+ people with 5 loaves of bread and 2 fish, giving sight to the blind, and many more - were all wonderful but a little scary for some.

Was he really who he said he was - The Messiah they've been waiting for for so many years? He didn't "fit" what many were expecting. He wasn't a worldly King, with a big army to take over by force.

After he was crucified, died, was raised to Life and taught them for 40 days before he ascended into the sky to Heaven one has to think they were wondering - "Now What?"

They knew what he said and yet what were they supposed to do?

This is where the Book of Acts starts - the Transition of Jesus handing over responsibility to the 11 Apostles - but, He didn't leave a pre-selected Management team who'd been trained in their respective roles. There was one Huge missing Component - the Spiritual **Power** needed to do the work he gave them. Of course that was the Holy Spirit.

Peter was never one to sit around and wait for things to happen. Remember, he walked on water and was the first to the empty tomb, etc. - so he addressed the people - 120 of them, including the Apostles. He was a man of Action and the Right man for launching the next phase of God's plan.

In Acts 1-12 we'll see how Jesus had prepared him and how The Holy Spirit Guided him to **Step Up in Faith** to Lead the new movement which became The Church.

It will be very exciting for each person who does this study to realize how Jesus has Prepared them for some specific ministry and then having the courage and confidence to **Step Up in Faith** and Obey! Yes, I'm talking to **You!**

Mark

A believer's **LifeMark** is the *legacy* left by a life spent *loving* and *serving* God and man.

LifeMark Ministries exists to help people discover that the Bible is *alive, active, and applicable.*
We help people *learn* God's Word so they can boldly *live* His Way...for His glory!
This is our calling and our passion. This is our LifeMark. What's yours?

To learn more about this ministry, visit our website: **www.LifeMarkMinistries.org**

Rob Pine joined LifeMark Ministries in January 2024 as Executive Director after serving Christian**Works** for Children for 17 years as Chief Executive Officer. There he provided direction, aligned resources, and created a safe loving environment for children and families to participate in a variety of programs to demonstrate God's goodness. Programs included licensed therapists and social workers to provide help for today, healing from the past and hope for tomorrow. Rob retired in 2006 as Executive Vice President of a Fortune 1000 company after a 36-year business career.

Involvement with church and ministry for Rob includes the blessing of teaching both youth and adult Bible study since 1977, expanding and encouraging disciples of Christ on numerous trips to Cambodia, Ghana, and Mexico, and serving as a church elder in Tuscaloosa, AL, and Garland, TX. He has also served in past years on the board of directors for YMCA, Dallas Christian School, Christian Care Centers, and Enterprise Christian Ministry.

In 1978 Rob was honorably discharged from the U.S. Army as Captain.

Rob has been married to Ellen since 1968. They have three children and five grandchildren.

Pastor **James Heffington** grew up in Grand Prairie, Texas where he came to know Christ as Savior at the age of 9. He sensed God's call to the ministry as a teenager and began pastoring while a student at Baylor. James earned a Bachelor of Arts in Religion from Baylor University as well as a Master of Divinity from Southwestern Baptist Theological Seminary. He has been a full-time pastor in Texas since 2000 and pastor at Masterpiece Church since May of 2012.

James is married to Kim and they have 2 children. God has blessed both Kim and James with many diverse opportunities to serve Him. James has served as a youth evangelist, worship leader and pastor.

How to Use This Study

This study is designed for group engagement; however, it is also effective for personal study. If used for personal study, email info@lifemarkministries.org for a PDF study guide and access to Video Talk.

Each week you will complete the lesson preparation and then meet with your small group to review your lesson and watch The Talk (on video). Start your lesson preparation with prayer, asking God to open your eyes to see the lessons He has for you.

Each lesson is structured identically with the following sections:

Questions - Answer these in preparation for each week's study.

Quotes - These sections will provide additional depth and context for your study.

Your Response - As you complete the lesson, spend some time reflecting on how you can personally apply what you have learned.

Prayer - Cultivating a strong prayer life helps you engage the power of the Holy Spirit to transform you.

Video Talk - Take notes as you listen to "The Talk." If in a group study, talk overviews may be provided by your group leader. If you need access to the videos, please email proof of purchase of this workbook to our office at: info@lifemarkministries.org

Keep in mind that this is a workbook, not a textbook. Don't be afraid to write in it, highlight it, circle key words — whatever it takes to help you absorb the content. We also recommend either purchasing a good Bible dictionary or using some online resources when you come across words or phrases with which you are not familiar. Here are a few web sites we recommend:

www.Bible.org

www.BlueLetterBible.org

www.GotQuestions.org

Before we get started, take a minute to write down what you hope to gain from this study:

_____

_____

_____

_____

Like anything, the more time and effort you invest in this study, the more you will grow in your walk with God. Most importantly, pray for God to guide you and for the Holy Spirit to reveal God's truth to you as you study and seek to apply His Word.

Table of Contents

Lesson 1: Introduction to the Book of Acts 2

Lesson 2: Jesus' Kingship and Command 6

Lesson 3: The Power of the Holy Spirit Arrives 12

Lesson 4: Undeniable Restoration and Refreshment... 18

Lesson 5: Challenge to Authority 24

Lesson 6: A New Community Under New Authority 30

Lesson 7: Men of Good Reputation, Full of the Spirit, and Wise 36

Lesson 8: The Gospel Spreads to Samaria and Ethiopia 42

Lesson 9: From Persecutor to Proclaimer... 48

Lesson 10: Turning Point, Controversy, and Expansion 54

Lesson 11: A Difficult Time for God's Glory 62

Citations Acts Church Foundation 69

Conclusion.. 71

Additional Resources.. 72

Lesson 1: Introduction to the Book of Acts

Questions: Acts Introduction

1. Who wrote the book of Acts? Acts 1:1, Luke 1:1-3, Acts 16:6 – 11.

2. Who was Luke writing to?

> "In writing Acts, Luke drew on written sources (15:23-29; 23:26-30), and he also, no doubt, interviewed key figures, such as Peter, John, and others in the Jerusalem church. Paul's two year imprisonment in Caesarea (24:27) gave Luke ample opportunity to interview Philip and his daughters (who were considered important sources of information on the early days of the church). Finally, Luke's frequent use of the first-person plural pronouns "we" and "us" (16:10-17; 20:5-21:18; 27:1-28:16) reveals that he was an eyewitness to many of the events recorded in Acts."
>
> John MacArthur[1]

3. What is the theme and purpose of the book of Acts? Acts 1:8.

4. Who are the two primary disciples of Jesus through whom Luke unfolds the early history of the church? Acts 2:14, 9:15-17.

5. What does Luke record as the major obstacles to the preaching and teaching of Jesus for the growth of the church? Acts 4:1-3, 12:1-3.

6. What is the role of the Holy Spirit in the book of Acts? Acts 1:8.

7. Acts is a historical account of the early church's beginning and expansion. What else does it record?

8. What problems did the early church face that we still must deal with today? Acts 2:44-45, 5:1-4, 6:1-4, 11:1-3, 12:1-2.

9. What do you know about the Apostle Peter?

10. What do you know about the Apostle Paul?

Your Response
What will you apply from this lesson that are practical steps you can take to release the power God has placed in you as a disciple of Christ, and in the family of believers you are a part of?

Prayer
Acknowledge God as _____.

Thank God for _____.

Ask God to transform you in a specific way more into the likeness of Christ by your study of His word in this lesson.

Specific ways from this lesson include _____.

Video Talk
Notes, comments and questions.

Lesson 2: Jesus' Kingship and Command

Questions: Acts Chapter 1

At his ascension to heaven, Jesus revealed His immediate plan for continuing His work and eternal vision for His church. Beginning with about 120 men and women disciples in Jerusalem, this led to the explosive growth by the power of the Holy Spirit to include all people on earth.

Read Acts 1:1-8

1. Why was it important for Jesus to present himself alive to the disciples? How did He convince them he was alive?

> "In the resurrection (and the ascension described in vv. 9-10), Jesus is indeed being enthroned as Israel's Messiah and therefore king of the whole world. The apostles must go out as heralds, not of someone who may become king at some point in the future, but of the one who has already been appointed and enthroned."
>
> — N. T. Wright[2]

2. Why were they to remain in Jerusalem? What had Jesus said God promised them? Where would it come from?

3. When was a time and circumstance that you had to wait on God?

4. What were his disciples most interested in learning from Jesus? How did Jesus respond to their question?

5. What did Jesus tell his disciples they were to be and to do? Why is it important? (Matthew 28:18-20).

6. Have you ever been a witness in a court proceeding? What does a witness do?

7. Where were the disciples to take their testimony?

Read Acts 1:9-11, Luke 24:50-51

1. What is the significance that a cloud received Jesus as He ascended into heaven? Read Exodus 14:19-24; 2 Chronicles 5:14; 1 Corinthians 10:1,2.

2. Where did the ascension take place?

3. What was Jesus doing for the disciples when He ascended?

4. Why were the two men in white clothing (angels) at the ascension? What did they tell the disciples?

5. **Do you think the disciples would have the picture portrayed in Daniel 7:13-14 in mind as they watched the ascension? Why or why not?**

Read Acts 1:12-26

1. **What was the disciple's response to Jesus' instructions and ascension? Who was included in this group of about 120 people?**

2. **Why did Peter think it was necessary to replace Judas? What criteria were put in place?**

3. **What did the disciples do to place the selection under the authority of the Lord?**

Your Response
What will you apply from this lesson that are practical steps you can take to release the power God has placed in you as a disciple of Christ, and in the family of believers you are a part of?

Prayer
Acknowledge God as _____.

Thank God for _____.

Ask God to transform you in a specific way more into the likeness of Christ by your study of His word in this lesson.

Specific ways from this lesson include _____.

Video Talk
Notes, comments and questions.

Lesson 3: The Power of the Holy Spirit Arrives

Questions: Acts Chapter 2

At the celebration of the annual Jewish festival, Pentecost, Jews of many languages from many cities, provinces, and nations were gathered to thank God for His provision of the harvest. The Holy Spirit manifests itself on Jesus' disciples this day, giving them the ability to speak in languages they did not know, appearing as tongues of fire. Peter delivers the first gospel message to this crowd and 3,000 believe the message, repent, are baptized, and receive the Holy Spirit.

Read Acts 2:1-13

1. What is the day of Pentecost?

2. Why would God choose this day for the apostles to be filled with the power of the Holy Spirit?

3. Describe the scene in the house where the disciples were gathered together.

4. What did it mean they could speak in tongues in Acts 2:4, 6-8 and 11? What did it not mean?

> "The Holy Spirit is mentioned in the book of Acts more than 50 times. Any attempted work of the church is doomed to failure without the Spirit (John 16:7-11)."
>
> David Jeremiah[3]

5. Describe the crowd's different responses.

Read Acts 2:14-21

1. How does Peter use Joel's prophecy to explain what is happening? Joel 2:28-32.

2. What should be the outcome of the pouring out of the Spirit on those in Christ in His church?

Read Acts 2:22-36

1. What specific truths does Peter proclaim about Jesus the crowd should know?

2. What evidence does Peter give in these Psalms that David is not talking about himself but is talking about Jesus? Psalms 16:8-11, Psalms 132:11, Psalms 110:1.

Read Acts 2:37 – 41

1. How did the crowd respond to Peter's message?

2. What did Peter tell them?

3. Who was the message of this promise for?

4. What were the 3,000 that were baptized added to?

Read Acts 2:42-47

1. What did this earliest group of believers in Jesus devote themselves to every day?

2. What does selling property and possessions to share with those in need mean?

3. Who added numbers to the church daily?

Your Response
What will you apply from this lesson that are practical steps you can take to release the power God has placed in you as a disciple of Christ, and in the family of believers you are a part of?

Prayer
Acknowledge God as _____.

Thank God for _____.

Ask God to transform you in a specific way more into the likeness of Christ by your study of His word in this lesson.

Specific ways from this lesson include _____.

Video Talk
Notes, comments and questions.

Lesson 4: Undeniable Restoration and Refreshment

Questions: Acts Chapter 3

The work of God, through the Spirit in the name of Jesus, moves to the gate leading to the temple where a no-name beggar, lame from birth, is healed to the wonder and amazement of the crowd. Peter healed him in the name of Jesus, which drew a crowd to hear Peter preach his second recorded gospel sermon, and many believed. The church now numbered 5,000 men.

Read Acts 3:1-11

1. How often was the lame man carried to the temple gate?

2. Why was it important to be there at the 9th hour?

3. What did the lame man hope and expect to receive from Peter and John?

4. What did Peter possess that he could give the lame man?

5. What was the lame man's response?

6. What was the temple crowd's response?

Read Acts 3:12-26

1. What was Peter's response to the crowd's reaction? Describe how God is at work in this event at the temple.

2. How does Peter describe Jesus in this sermon?

3. What words does Peter use to convict the crowd of their sin against God?

4. What role in the redemption story does Peter say the prophets play? Read Isaiah 53 as an example.

5. What did Peter tell the crowd they should do?

6. What are the results of repentance and turning to God?

7. Who is the prophet like Moses, God raised up? Why should His words be listened to and obeyed?

8. Why did God raise up His servant, Jesus, first to the Israelites?

9. Would there be a second group?

Your Response
What will you apply from this lesson that are practical steps you can take to release the power God has placed in you as a disciple of Christ, and in the family of believers you are a part of?

Prayer
Acknowledge God as _____.

Thank God for _____.

Ask God to transform you in a specific way more into the likeness of Christ by your study of His word in this lesson.

Specific ways from this lesson include _____.

Video Talk
Notes, comments and questions.

23

Lesson 5: Challenge to Authority

Questions: Acts Chapter 4

The authority of the Jewish elders, priests, and scribes, known as the Sanhedrin, faced a challenge to their authority from the apostles. They were accused of rejecting and condemning the very Messiah prophesied by the prophets. The Sanhedrin attempted to stop the apostles from preaching, teaching in the name of Jesus, but their response not only failed, but promoted the spread of the name of Jesus as the Messiah.

Read Acts 4:1-12

1. Why were the priest, captain of the temple guard, and Sadducees greatly disturbed, upset, and angry?

2. How long had Peter and John been at the temple?

> "Chief Priests, Rulers, Elders, and Scribes: These positions made up the Sanhedrin, the Jewish national ruling body and supreme court. It had 71 members, including the High Priest. The chief priest were a group within the Sanhedrin composed of members of influential priestly families. They were mostly Sadducees. The scribes were primarily Pharisees and were the authorities on Jewish law."
>
> John MacArthur[4]

3. What was the result of the teaching and preaching of the message?

4. What was the big question the rulers, elders, and scribes (Sanhedrin) wanted an answer to?

5. Describe how Peter was able to respond to the authorities' question so boldly. Read John 14:26.

6. What was Peter's response and charge against the rulers?

7. How did Peter describe the exclusivity of Jesus?

Read Acts 4:13-22

1. What did the Sanhedrin (priests, rulers, and elders) recognize about Peter and John?

2. What was the Sanhedrin's dilemma? How did they try to solve it?

3. How did Peter and John respond to their threats?

Read Acts 4:23-31

1. Why did the disciples mention David and quote Psalms 2:1 and 2 in their prayer? Who did they credit for David's words in the Psalm?

2. What did the disciples ask God for in their prayer? What did they not pray for?

3. What happened after they prayed?

Read Acts 4:32-37

1. What characterized the believers' thoughts, words, and actions as being filled with the Holy Spirit?

2. Describe how Barnabas is introduced by Luke and known by the disciples in Jerusalem.

3. Why do we need to know this about Barnabus?

Your Response
What will you apply from this lesson that are practical steps you can take to release the power God has placed in you as a disciple of Christ, and in the family of believers you are a part of?

Prayer
Acknowledge God as _____.

Thank God for _____.

Ask God to transform you in a specific way more into the likeness of Christ by your study of His word in this lesson.

Specific ways from this lesson include _____.

Video Talk
Notes, comments and questions.

Lesson 6: A New Community Under New Authority

Questions: Acts Chapter 5

The community of believers was functioning as God intended to the point that the Jewish officials (the Sanhedrin) were losing the respect of the people for their position as religious authority. The Holy Spirit was working signs and wonders through the apostles that drew crowds to hear the gospel and establish the apostle's authority in the rapidly growing church.

Read Acts 5:1-11

1. What is the difference between the gift from the sale of property by Barnabas in Acts 4:37 and the sale of property by Ananias and Sapphira?

2. How did Ananias and Sapphira lie to the Holy Spirit?

3. Why did Peter ask if the property before it was sold, and the money received after it, was under their control?

> "When he (Satan) failed to destroy the early church, he tried to infiltrate and hinder it by prompting people to live in insincere and hypocritical ways. He still uses such tactics today."
>
> — David Jeremiah[5]

4. How did God respond to the actions of Ananias and Sapphira? What was the response of the believers and all who heard about it?

5. Describe why you think God's judgment was so swift and severe for Ananias and Sapphira?

Read Acts 5:12 – 16

1. What was the purpose of the signs and wonders by the apostles?

2. Why would those not in their company, gathering at Solomon's porch, not want to associate with them but hold them in high esteem?

3. How was it that more and more men and women were added to the believers?

Read Acts 5:17 - 42

1. Why were the apostles arrested and put in jail?

2. What did the angel of the Lord tell them to do after he released them from prison, and what did they do?

3. Why was the Sanhedrin so angry and distressed with the apostles?

4. Describe the apostle's response to the Sanhedrin.

5. How did the Sanhedrin respond to the apostle's message?

6. What was Gamaliel's wise counsel?

7. How did the apostles respond to the punishment of flogging?

Your Response
What will you apply from this lesson that are practical steps you can take to release the power God has placed in you as a disciple of Christ, and in the family of believers you are a part of?

Prayer
Acknowledge God as _____.

Thank God for _____.

Ask God to transform you in a specific way more into the likeness of Christ by your study of His word in this lesson.

Specific ways from this lesson include _____.

Video Talk
Notes, comments and questions.

Lesson 7: Men of Good Reputation, Full of the Spirit, and Wise

Questions: Acts Chapters 6 and 7

Church growth created issues for the early church. A particular group, Hellenistic widows, in the church in Jerusalem were underserved. The apostle's wisdom called for the people of the church to solve the problem by selecting men of specific character to serve in a special capacity. One of the men, Stephen, was called upon by God to be the first martyr of the church, setting the stage for the church to expand outside of Jerusalem.

Read Acts 6:1 – 7

1. What was the dispute the apostles needed to address among the believers as they experienced dramatic growth in their numbers?

> "The "Hebrews" or "Hebraic Jews" mentioned in verse 1 referred to the early Christians from this first group. The "Hellenist" or "Grecian Jews" were Christians from the second group who had returned to Jerusalem after years or perhaps generations away."
>
> N. T. Wright[6]

2. How did the apostles resolve the complaint of the Hellenistic widows?

3. Why did the apostles not take over the work to resolve the complaint themselves?

4. What were the requirements for selecting the men to take on the work of distributing food to the Hellenistic widows?

5. What was the result of the apostle's solution to the issue of distribution of food?

Read Acts 6: 8 – 15

1. Stephen, one of the seven, was also busy doing what in Jerusalem?

2. What did Stephen's Jewish adversaries accuse him of?

3. Why are they angry?

4. How was Stephen able to argue successfully against those that opposed him? (Read Luke 21:12 – 19).

5. What did they do?

6. How would you describe Stephen's face, "like the face of an angel"? What does this phrase communicate?

Read Acts 7:1 – 53

1. Why did Stephen recount the history of the Jews to the scribes, elders, and Sadducees?

> "the host of heaven. These were presumably astral deities of various kinds as well as "Molech" and "Raphan". The quotation from Amos 5:25-27 is a damning indictment of a period that many Jews must have seen as in some ways the honeymoon period between God and Israel. It was in fact, says Amos (and Stephen), a time of rank rebellion, of idolatry rather than true worship."
>
> — N. T. Wright[7]

2. What did Stephen say in conclusion that infuriated them?

Read Acts 7:54 – 60

1. What did Stephen tell his accusers and the Sanhedrin he saw in heaven?

2. How were Stephen's last words an example of Jesus? (Read Luke 23:34, 46).

3. What can you learn from Stephen's example?

Your Response

What will you apply from this lesson that are practical steps you can take to release the power God has placed in you as a disciple of Christ, and in the family of believers you are a part of?

Prayer

Acknowledge God as _____.

Thank God for _____.

Ask God to transform you in a specific way more into the likeness of Christ by your study of His word in this lesson.

Specific ways from this lesson include _____.

Video Talk

Notes, comments and questions.

Lesson 8: The Gospel Spreads to Samaria and Ethiopia

Questions: Acts Chapter 8

The Biblical record often relates how God uses what is evil intended to go against His purpose, He uses to accomplish His purpose. God's ability to use all things for His glory is demonstrated in the story of Philip's activity after the death of Stephen and following the persecution of the church. Powered by the Holy Spirit, Philip preaches and teaches the gospel, opening the doors of the church to Samaritans and an official of the Queen of Ethiopia.

Read Acts 8: 1 – 4

1. How did God work for His good purpose in the death of Stephen and the actions of Saul? Read Acts 1:8.

> "The persecution, which seemed to be negative, was in reality a positive factor. It led to the first great missionary outreach by the early church. Satan's attempt to stamp out the fire merely scattered the embers and started new fires around the world. In the words of the early church Father Tertullian, the blood of the martyrs became the seed of the church."
>
> John MacArthur[8]

2. Describe Saul.

3. What did the disciples who were scattered throughout Judea and Samaria do?

Read Acts 8:5 – 25

1. What did Philip do in Samaria?

2. How did the Samaritans respond to Philips' preaching and healing?

3. What is the purpose of the apostle Peter and John's visit to Samaria?

4. Considering the historic deep antipathy between the Samaritans and Jews, what is God's message revealed in this event?

5. Why did Simon believe, be baptized, and follow Philip around?

6. What was Simon really after? Why did Peter so strongly rebuke him?

Read Acts 8:26 – 40

1. From Samaria, where was Philip's next assignment? Who was giving him his assignment?

2. What was puzzling the Ethiopian eunuch in the scriptures we know as Isaiah 53, as he was traveling?

3. How did Philip approach the Ethiopian eunuch?

4. What was the Ethiopian eunuch's response to Philip's teaching?

5. From the desert road to Gaza, where was Philip's next preaching and teaching assignment and who took him there?

6. What do you find the most admirable character traits of Philip?

Your Response

What will you apply from this lesson that are practical steps you can take to release the power God has placed in you as a disciple of Christ, and in the family of believers you are a part of?

Prayer

Acknowledge God as _____.

Thank God for _____.

Ask God to transform you in a specific way more into the likeness of Christ by your study of His word in this lesson.

Specific ways from this lesson include _____.

Video Talk

Notes, comments and questions.

Lesson 9: From Persecutor to Proclaimer

Questions: Acts Chapter 9

The conversion and transformation of a Pharisee, Saul of Tarsus, from a lead persecutor of the disciples of Christ to the lead proclaimer of the gospel of Christ. This event is so significant for Luke that it is told three times. First, here in Acts 9, then from Paul himself, recorded by Luke in chapters 22 and 26 of Acts.

Read Acts 9:1 – 19

1. Why was Saul going on a 200-mile trip from Jerusalem to Damascus?

2. What happened to Saul as he neared Damascus?

3. How did Saul get to Damascus and what did he do when he arrived?

4. Who is Ananias? Read Acts 22:12-18.

5. Why did Ananias hesitate to obey Jesus' command to go to where Saul was staying?

6. What happened when Ananias met Saul at the house of Judas, on Straight Street?

7. Take a moment and recall when the truth of Jesus was revealed to you. Jot down a few notes and share if comfortable.

8. How did Ananias following Jesus' instruction, play a role in changing the church?

9. Describe a time when you have been hesitant to follow God's command, but you followed through like Ananias. What was the result?

Read Acts 9:20 – 31

1. What was Saul's immediate response for several days in Damascus?

2. How many days elapsed in verse 23, when the Jews began their plot to kill Saul? Read Galatians 1:15 – 19.

> "After narrowly escaping from Damascus with his life, Paul spent three years in Nabatean Arabia, south and east of the Dead Sea (Gal. 1:17,18). During that time, he received much of his doctrine as direct revelation from the Lord. More than any other individual, Paul was responsible for the spread of Christianity throughout the Roman Empire."
>
> John MacArthur[9]

3. What happened when Saul returned to Jerusalem?

4. What was the result of all this activity for the church throughout Galilee, Samaria, and Judea?

Read Acts 9:32 – 43

1. What was the result of the miracles of healing Aeneas in Lydda and the resurrection of Tabitha in Joppa, through the power of the Holy Spirit, by Peter? What does this tell you about the purpose of these miracles?

2. Why is Peter's stay with Simon, a tanner, significant?

Your Response

What will you apply from this lesson that are practical steps you can take to release the power God has placed in you as a disciple of Christ, and in the family of believers you are a part of?

Prayer

Acknowledge God as _____.

Thank God for _____.

Ask God to transform you in a specific way more into the likeness of Christ by your study of His word in this lesson.

Specific ways from this lesson include _____.

Video Talk
Notes, comments and questions.

Lesson 10: Turning Point, Controversy, and Expansion

Questions: Acts Chapters 10 and 11

A watershed moment for the church occurred at the home of a Gentile Roman Centurian named Cornelius. Upon hearing the Gentiles had believed the word of God, some Jewish believers in Jerusalem confronted Peter for having been in a Gentile home and eating with them. Peter related the story, and all objections were settled with this group. A division in the church over this issue would grow into a major problem in years to follow. At the scattering of the believers from Jerusalem, a church was established in Antioch with a great number of people including Gentiles of the Greek culture and custom. Barnabus and Saul began to minister together in Antioch where the disciples were first called Christians.

Read Acts 10:1 – 7

1. How is Cornelius described by Luke?

2. Why did the angel visit Cornelius in a vision?

3. What did the angel tell Cornelius to do?

Read Acts 10:8 – 22

1. What experience did Peter have on the roof of Simon's house at noon?

2. Why did Peter recoil at the idea? Read Leviticus 11.

3. What is the meaning of the angel's words to "Not declare anything impure that God has made clean"?

4. Who sent the three men to Peter to bring him to Joppa?

5. What is significant about Peter inviting a Roman soldier and two Gentile servants to be guests at Simon's house?

Read Acts 10:23 – 48

1. Why was it necessary for Peter and some additional believers to go to Cornelius's house in Joppa?

2. What happened while Peter was speaking?

> "Peter and those with him (circumcised, that is, Jewish, men) need to know that these uncircumcised people have been regarded by the Holy Spirit as fit vessels to be filled with his presence and voice. And if that is so, there can be no barriers to baptism. All this is what is meant by the opening line of Peter's speech, "God has no favorites"."
>
> N. T. Wright[10]

3. What was Peter's response to the Gentiles speaking in tongues?

Read Acts 11:1 - 18

1. Why did the Jewish believers in Christ have an issue with Peter and his experience in Joppa?

2. Why would Luke, inspired by the Spirit, record a second time the story of what happened at Cornelius's house?

3. What did the voice from heaven mean when it told Peter, "Do not call anything impure that God has made clean."?

4. What did Peter possess that devout Cornelius, his family, and his household needed to be saved? See Acts 10:43.

5. What convinced Peter that he told his Jewish believer critics that God granted repentance that leads to life to the Gentiles?

Read Acts 11:19 – 30

1. What was the result of the persecution of the church in Jerusalem beginning with the death of Stephen?

2. What happened differently in Antioch?

3. How did the church in Jerusalem respond when they heard about the Antioch church?

4. Describe Barnabas's reaction and action when he arrived in Antioch.

5. How can you encourage people in their faith today?

6. Why did Barnabas go to Tarsus and bring Saul back to Antioch?

7. What name did the disciples in the church at Antioch call themselves?

> "In the midst of the growth of the church in Antioch, followers of Christ – Jews and Gentiles – were first called Christians ... The reason is not exactly clear, but some scholars believe "Christian" at first was a derogatory term; a nickname of sorts... The word is only used three times in the New Testament, each time with a derisive connotation (Acts 11:26; 26:28; 1 Peter 4:16). What likely began as a derogatory term was embraced as early as the second century as a term of endearment then and today for those who follow Jesus of Nazareth."
>
> David Jeremiah[11]

8. What is the significance that the disciples that started the church in Antioch are not named, only identified by where they came from? Is it significant that the disciples in Antioch just called themselves Christians?

9. How did the disciples at Antioch display their concern for all disciples of Jesus?

60

Your Response

What will you apply from this lesson that are practical steps you can take to release the power God has placed in you as a disciple of Christ, and in the family of believers you are a part of?

Prayer

Acknowledge God as _____.

Thank God for _____.

Ask God to transform you in a specific way more into the likeness of Christ by your study of His word in this lesson.

Specific ways from this lesson include _____.

Video Talk

Notes, comments and questions.

Lesson 11: *A Difficult Time for God's Glory*

Questions: Acts Chapters 12

At this point, Luke brings to Theophilus and all readers an inside look at the hearts and minds of the disciples 10 to 11 years after the death and resurrection of Jesus. A persecuted group of people yet continuing to add to their number. A praying group of people yet wondering if God can answer. A faithful group of people yet their faith at times is weak. An ordinary group of people yet powered by the Spirit used by God to accomplish His extraordinary purpose.

Read Acts 12:1-19

1. How does Herod Agrippa 1 persecute the Church?

> "The full name of the king in Acts 12 is Herod Julius Agrippa, and he is sometimes referred to as Agrippa I in distinction to his son, Herod Agrippa II, whom we shall meet in Acts 25-26. Herod Agrippa I died in 44 A. D. as we know from various sources."
>
> N. T. Wright[12]

2. Why does he put Peter in prison?

3. What is the church's response to Peter's imprisonment?

4. Describe how Peter was secured in the prison to ensure there is no escape.

5. Why is it so difficult for the disciples gathered to pray at the home of Mary, to believe Peter is at the door?

6. In relating the miraculous story of his escape, who did Peter give the credit to?

7. What did Peter instruct the disciples to do?

8. What is King Herod Agrippa's response to Peter's escape?

Read Acts 12:20-25

1. How would you describe the character of King Herod Agrippa 1?

2. What was God's response to King Agrippa 1 thoughts, words, and deeds after he addressed publicly the people of Tyre and Sidon?

3. What was the result of King Herod Agrippa's persecution of the church?

Concluding Questions on Acts Chapters 1 – 12

1. List some highlights of Peter's ministry in Chapters 1 – 12. Why did Luke, led by the Spirit, single out these to be recorded, covering the first 10 to 11 years of church history?

2. What lessons can the 21st-century church of Jesus Christ learn about its mission and purpose from the church of the first century?

Your Response
What will you apply from this lesson that are practical steps you can take to release the power God has placed in you as a disciple of Christ, and in the family of believers you are a part of?

Prayer
Acknowledge God as _____.

Thank God for _____.

Ask God to transform you in a specific way more into the likeness of Christ by your study of His word in this lesson.

Specific ways from this lesson include _____.

Video Talk
Notes, comments and questions.

Citations Acts Church Foundation

[1] John MacArthur, *Acts: The Spread of the Gospel*, Thomas Nelson, 2007, page 1

[2] N. T. Wright, *Acts: 24 Studies for Individuals and Groups,* Intervarsity Press, 2010, page 12

[3] David Jeremiah, *The Jeremiah Study Bible: NKJV,* Worthy Publishing, 2013, page 1486

[4] John MacArthur, *Acts: The Spread of the Gospel*, Thomas Nelson, 2007, page 14

[5] David Jeremiah, *The Jeremiah Study Bible: NKJV,* Worthy Publishing, 2013, page 1494

[6] N. T. Wright, *Acts: 24 Studies for Individuals and Groups,* Intervarsity Press, 2010, page 36

[7] N. T. Wright, *Acts: 24 Studies for Individuals and Groups,* Intervarsity Press, 2010, page 43

[8] John MacArthur, *Acts: The Spread of the Gospel,* Thomas Nelson, 2007, page 35

[9] John MacArthur, *Acts: The Spread of the Gospel,* Thomas Nelson, 2007, page 46

[10] N. T. Wright, *Acts: 24 Studies for Individuals and Groups,* Intervarsity Press, 2010, page 57

[11] David Jeremiah, *The Jeremiah Study Bible: NKJV,* Worthy Publishing, 2013, page 1507

[12] N. T. Wright, *Acts: 24 Studies for Individuals and Groups,* Intervarsity Press, 2010, page 65

Congratulations!

You have completed this study of God's Word – great job! We pray that you have been challenged by what you have learned, have grown closer to the Lord and His family of believers, and have applied His Word in your life.

It's important that you don't stop now! Here are some suggestions to help you continue to grow:

Daily Prayer: Continue the habit of starting each day with prayer. It's a conversation between you and God. Talk with Him about your day. Praise Him and share your concerns. Ask Him to fill you with His Spirit and guide your decisions each day. Strive to keep Him at the forefront of your thoughts.

Daily Bible Reading: It is invaluable to be in God's Word on a daily basis. We recommend spending some time in the four gospels to learn about who Jesus is and what he taught. Also, the wonderful books of Psalms and Proverbs are full of practical wisdom you can apply in your life.

Continuing study in Acts, Chapters 13-28: January 2025 our study in Acts continues with a new workbook: The Church's Expansion: Paul Steps Out in Faith covering Acts chapters 13-28. Contact us to join a group, start a group, or do a personal study at info@LifeMarkMinistries.org.

Start Another Study: We have a variety of studies available, some are showcased on the following pages, including *Dive In!* which will take you across the breadth and into the depths of God's Word, as well as an in-depth study on the Holy Spirit called *Fire Up!*. There are also a number of excellent Bible studies available at your local Christian bookstore or online. Regardless of which one you select, the important thing is to continue to study His Word!

Visit our Website: There you will find additional studies, tips, encouragement and resources to help you in your walk with God. **www.LifeMarkMinistries.org**

Sign-up for Mondays with Mark: Our weekly video devotional will help you begin your week in God's Word. These short videos arrive in your email inbox every Monday morning. To learn more, visit **www.MondaysWithMark.org**

His House: To study the Bible in an innovative way for life transforming guidance, purchase a year long Bible study guide, completed on your own personal time and schedule. After an introductory series of lessons, you choose the study that is currently applicable to you. Studies are four-minute videos with downloads of questions, challenges and tools addressing subjects like does God exist, what is the Bible, Personal Health, Addictions, Family Relationships, and Government and Christians among many others. You will find what you are looking for in over 250 lessons.

We would love to hear from you! Please send your thoughts and feedback on this study to us by emailing: **info@lifemarkministries.org**. Share how this study has impacted your life and what you have learned through it.

LIFEMARK
MINISTRIES

Additional Resources by LIFEMARK MINISTRIES

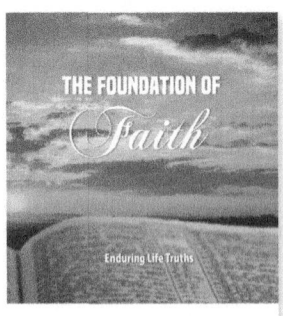

Foundation of Faith: Enduring Life Truths

Have you ever wondered about how or why our world was created? Or been confused about what the Bible tells you and what you read or hear elsewhere? Have your Christian beliefs been challenged by things you hear and read?

Biblical foundational truths are being challenged at all levels of society, government, business, education, entertainment and even the Church! We don't have all the answers but we do have God's Word.

The **first eleven chapters of Genesis** includes many biblical truths that must be part of the foundation of our faith. Our new study, Foundation of Faith, covers these eleven chapters and will help you to review and renew your commitment to God and to His Word by addressing the lies and deceptions we are bombarded with daily.

This 10-week study will review many truths you already know, and dive deeper on topics that are being challenged today, so that you can be sure your foundation is solidly supported by God's Word. This study will strengthen your beliefs and resolve to be God's faithful ambassadors for His glory and the benefit of others based on the truths God has put in the Bible. Get started today.

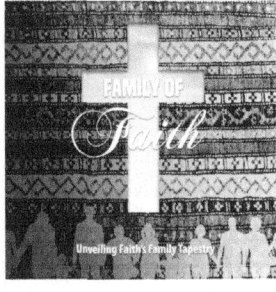

Family of Faith: Unveiling of Faith's Family Tapestry

God's plan for mankind is rich in complexity and design, just as ancient tapestries are. This study continues in Genesis where our *The Foundation of Faith* study left off. This study through **Genesis chapters 12-50** will show us how God continued His plan and love story for mankind by designing and developing a **Family of Faith**.

In this 16-week study we will weave our way through the threads of this family's rich history and see how God ensures His will is done. Chosen although flawed people struggle to follow His plan. Sin is ever-present. But then as today, God protects, provides and forgives which makes this study incredibly powerful and relevant to our world today.

Through this Family of Faith we will learn the importance of trust and obedience to God's plan and purposes for us and how God never fails to keep His promises. See how you belong in His Family of Faith. Get started today.

Dive In! Explore the Breadth and Depth of God's Story

Do you desire to have a better understanding of the story of God's Word? Do you wonder how the stories of the Bible fit in the context of history? Do you find yourself wishing you knew the characters of the Bible better?

This 28-week Bible study will take you across the breadth and into the depths of God's Word. You'll gain a better understanding of the context for individual books and how they are interconnected. You'll discover how the activities in the heavenly realm affect the earthly realm. You'll grow more confident in your faith as you see prophecies fulfilled. You'll learn lessons from Biblical characters' victories and defeats. You'll grasp the significant roles of Israel and the Church in God's amazing story of redemption.

Through it all, you'll gain a broader and yet more personal view of God, Jesus, and the Holy Spirit, and you'll develop a greater appreciation for the depth of God's unfathomable LOVE for YOU!

Fire Up! A Bible Study of God's Holy Spirit

Do you have questions about the Holy Spirit? Do you know what the Bible says about Him? Are you fully engaging His power in your life? Most believers struggle with really understanding who or what the Holy Spirit is. Instead of that driving us to learn more, we pull away because we're uncomfortable with what we don't know. It's human nature! But if you've placed your faith in Jesus Christ as your personal Savior, then you actually have the Holy Spirit living inside of you! *Don't you think it's time to introduce yourself and get to know Him better?*

This 24-week study will help you grow deeper in your relationship with God the Father as you study the person, presence and power of His Spirit. The Holy Spirit can be a difficult, complicated, and sometimes divisive topic, but at the same time, He is a priceless gift from God! Don't miss this opportunity to grow more intimate with a holy God through His Holy Spirit.

Mindshift: Changing Your Direction - A Study of the Sermon on the Mount

Have you ever studied the greatest sermon ever told? Have you wondered why Jesus describes the "blessed" life with a viewpoint that is opposite the world's viewpoint? Have you struggled knowing how to live the transformed life of a Christian?

In this 8-week journey through the Sermon on the Mount **(Matt 5-7)**, you will have a greater understanding of the two paths offered in life: the path that leads to everlasting destruction and the path that leads to eternal life. You will be prompted to think differently about the Christian life and encouraged to be salt and light in a dark world. You will have a greater appreciation for the righteousness that Christ offers and desire to live differently through the power of the Holy Spirit in you.

The Sermon on the Mount shifted the minds of Jesus' followers away from the legalism and hypocrisy of those who abused the law to focus on the invitation to follow the One who would ***fulfill*** the law. He offers the same invitation to you — eternal life by grace through faith, resulting in a life dedicated to serving Him out of love and gratitude. Will you accept His invitation and follow?

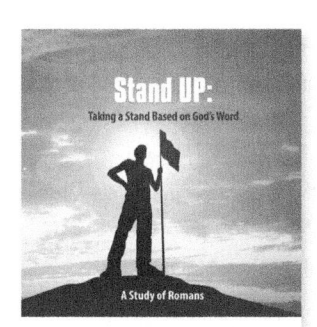

Stand UP: Taking a Stand Based on God's Word - A Study of Romans

Do you struggle with discouragement in a world that seems to have lost its foundation? Do you desire to make a difference but aren't sure what to say to combat the lies in our declining culture? Do you sometimes find yourself knowing what you believe but you're unsure why you believe it?

Things that most of us never even considered in the past have become common place today —they are friction points in our everyday lives. The only way to counteract these falsehoods is to know the truth as found in God's Word, the Bible.

This 26-week study will dive deep into the book of Romans, a letter written by the Apostle Paul to the believers in Rome. You will learn truths about a wide variety of topics that affect society even today, and you will be more confident as a result of knowing the truth so you can boldly and graciously Stand UP for God. Get started today.

Additional Resources by LIFEMARK MINISTRIES

Aging with Honor: A Practical Guide to Help You Honor Your Parents as They Age

Growing up is hard to do. That's why God gave kids parents — to teach, train, help, and guide them as they go from having a lot of limitations to having a lot of freedoms and into adulthood.

Growing old is even harder. That's why God gave parents kids — to encourage, support, help, and guide them as they go from having a lot of freedoms to having a lot of limitations.

This practical guide will cover a variety of issues in five individual segments: Financial Needs, Medical Needs, Logistical Needs, Relational Needs, and Spiritual Needs. It will provide you with the tools and resources that you will need in order to evaluate your situation and create a plan that works best for your family.

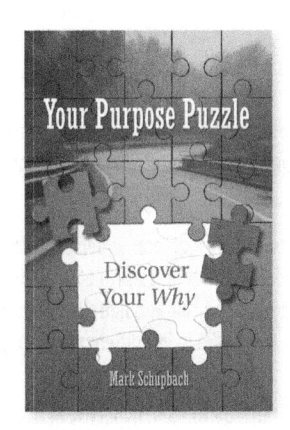

Your Purpose Puzzle: Discover Your *Why*

Ponder your life for a moment.

Why are you living in your town? Why do you have the job you have? Why are you in a specific relationship? Why are you living in your current conditions, whatever they might be? God has a purpose for everyone — a purpose that He determined for us before we were even born. He created us specifically for this purpose. We rarely see the full picture, but God gradually reveals pieces of it over time. It is our job to assemble the puzzle and faithfully carry out our purpose. This guide will walk you through the process of prayerfully evaluating your God-given purpose and pursuing it!

What Makes a Person Truly Rich?

To answer that you have first to determine what things have real value. No doubt there is a financial component. However, that component is not net worth as much as it is adequate income for life.

In addition to income, how you spend your time is critical. Of course, having good health influences how much freedom you have with your time and what contribution you make. Lastly, think about all the times in your life that have given you the most joy. Did they revolve around key relationships in your life?

Combining these factors, I submit that a truly rich person is rich because they have **meaningful Relationships, adequate Income, are making a meaningful Contribution, and are blessed with good Health.**

Below are a few general principles, some "RICH Realities," to keep in mind before we begin:

1. Someone else will always have more _____ than you do. Don't make life a contest!
2. Don't worry – especially about the things you cannot control.
3. Regardless of how well you plan, it will likely turn out differently – and that is okay. It is still important to plan!
4. What the world says we need is usually wrong. Self-worth is greater than net worth!

With these in mind, let's take a closer look at each of the four components of a truly RICH life.

www.LifeMarkMinistries.org
info@LifeMarkMinistries.org
972-619-5434
Facebook.com/LifeMarkMinistries

Made in the USA
Middletown, DE
04 August 2024